Renewal Myths and Rites
of the
Primitive Hunters and Planters

The Eranos Lectures Series

RENEWAL MYTHS AND RITES
OF THE
PRIMITIVE HUNTERS AND PLANTERS

Joseph Campbell

Spring Publications, Inc.
Dallas, Texas

Published 1989 by Spring Publications, Inc.; P.O. Box 222069; Dallas, Texas 75222
Printed in the United States of America

Series cover design by Maribeth Lipscomb and Patricia Mora
This cover produced by Shannon Everett

International Distributors:
Spring; Postfach; 8803 Rüschlikon; Switzerland.
Japan Spring Sha, Inc.; 12–10, 2-Chome, Nigawa Takamaru; Takarazuka 665, Japan.
Element Books Ltd; Longmead Shaftesbury; Dorset SP7 8PL; England.
Astam Books Pty. Ltd.; 27B Llewellyn St.; Balmain, Sydney, N.S.W. 2041; Australia.
Libros e Imagenes; Apdo. Post 40–085; México D.F. 06140; México.

Library of Congress Cataloging-in-Publication Data
Campbell, Joseph, 1904–
Renewal myths and rites of the primitive hunters and
planters.
(The Eranos lectures series, ISSN 0743-586X ; 9)
Bibliography: p.
1. Death—Mythology. 2. Rites and ceremonies—
Cross-cultural studies. 3. Society, Primitive.
I. Title. II. Series.
BL325.D35C36 1989   291'.042   88–35575
ISBN 0-88214-409-X

Eranos Lectures Series: ISSN 0743-586X

Acknowledgments
"Renewal Myths and Rites of the Primitive Hunters and Planters" was
a lecture presented originally at the 1959 Eranos Conference in Ascona,
Switzerland, and appeared in the *Eranos Jahrbuch 28—1959* (Ascona:
Eranos Foundation), pp. 407–57. It is published here with the kind per-
mission of the Eranos Foundation in agreement with the author's heirs.

I.

I wonder how many of you know that the earliest unquestionable evidence of mythology and ritual has been found precisely in this part of the world: Switzerland and the German Alps.

High in the peaks around St. Gallen, Emil Bächler discovered and excavated, from 1903 to 1927, three extremely interesting caves: Wild-kirchli, Drachenloch, and Wildmannlisloch[1]. Within these, at a depth of about six feet beneath the present surface of the floor, little walls of stone were encountered, some thirty-two inches high, forming bins or storage areas, within which a number of cave-bear skulls were preserved. Some of these skulls had circles of stones arranged around them; others were set upon stone slabs; one had the leg bones of a cave bear (perhaps its own) placed beneath its snout; another had the leg bones pushed through its eyes. Obviously, in some very early period these relics had been associated with a cult. There were flagstone floorings on the level of the bins, stone benches and worktables, flints of an extremely early, pre-Mousterian type, charcoal (indicating the use of fire) and a number of altars: the earliest altars yet found anywhere in the world, and the earliest evidence of the use of fire yet unearthed in Europe.

---

[1] EMIL BÄCHLER, *Das alpine Paläolithikum der Schweiz*, Basel 1940.

For the cave bear has been extinct for the past thirty or forty thousand years—since the close of the last glacial age, the Würm glaciation. Moreover, all of the caves were at such a height that they could not have been entered during the period of the great cold. The first two were about seven thousand feet and the last over eight thousand feet above sea level. During the centuries of the Würm they were completely under ice. Therefore, those cave-bear skulls were stored away *before* the coming of the last ice age: during the earlier, comparatively warm period of the Riss-Würm Interglacial, which is to be dated, approximately, between 75,000 and 200,000 B.C.

The German evidence was investigated independently of the Swiss in central Franconia, near Velden, in a cave called Petershöhle, by Konrad Hörmann, during the years from 1916 to 1922; and here again, the objects preserved were the skulls and leg bones of the cave bear. Five such skulls had been placed in closet-like recesses in the walls, about a hundred thousand years ago[2].

Nothing earlier in the way of a sacred site has yet been identified anywhere on earth. The period is considerably earlier than that of the great Cro-Magnon caves of southern France and northern Spain, which are definitely post-glacial. Nor had the human race yet evolved to the status of *homo sapiens*. The hands that stored those skulls away were of an earlier, far less attractive creature known as Neanderthal Man *(homo Neanderthalensis)*.

His was an age when the countryside of Europe was not at all as it is today. England and Ireland were part of the mainland and great rivers flowed through the valleys that are now the Irish Sea, the North Sea, and English Channel—rivers to which the Thames, Seine, Garonne, and even the Rhine were but tributaries. And what is now the strait of Gibraltar was then a land bridge connecting Africa and Europe, while Italy and Sicily stretched in a broad, irregular mass to the southern mainland—so that what is now the Mediterranean was then two inland lakes. The elephant, southern mammoth, broad-nosed rhinoceros and

---

[2] KONRAD HÖRMANN, *Die Petershöhle bei Velden in Mittelfranken,* "Abhandlungen der Naturhistorischen Gesellschaft zu Nürnberg", 1923.

hippopotamus ranged in a landscape more tropical than that of modern Europe. Lions stalked the bison, aurochs, and giant deer. And presently, as the cold of the coming glacial age began to press down from Scandinavia and a sheet of ice, covering the whole Baltic, crept southward to envelop northern Germany while the ice caps of the Alps reached down some 2,000 feet below their present level, over the tundras and cold steppe-lands, the musk ox, woolly mammoth and woolly rhinoceros appeared; herds of reindeer, also, and the arctic fox. The cave lion, cave leopard, and great cave hyena stalked their prey. Herds of wild horses, cattle, and bison grazed upon a plain that stretched far eastward, into Asia. And the vigorous Neanderthalers, remaining in those dangerous regions, ran down and slaughtered even the woolly mammoth, not with arrows—for the bow and arrow had not yet been invented—but with clubs, heavy rocks, and pointed sticks. They had to press close in for such a kill, and the work required a man's skill and strength as well as courage[3].

It was therefore the male, and not the female, upon whom the whole life and substance of the little hunting bands depended. Animal food was their staple; animal skins provided warmth; animal sinews were their ropes; animal teeth and claws their ornaments. There is reason to believe (as we shall see) that the magical energy of woman was utilized in the rituals of that long age of the early hunt; but it was through the male that the life-sustaining benefits finally came, and the male point of view, the male force, the male mode of experiencing life, death, and renewal was the ultimate determinant in the myths and rituals of those primitive votaries of the Great Hunt and the Master Bear.

It is, then, to such an age that these Alpine sanctuaries are to be referred.

And the earliest *human* burials of which we have knowledge are also of that remote age of Neanderthal Man; for example: the skeleton of a youth of about seventeen reposing in a sleeping posture, pillowed on a pile of flint, with a beautiful stone hand-axe at his side and the charred, split bones of wild cattle round about, interred in a cave in southern

---

[3] HENRY FAIRFIELD OSBORN, *Men of the Old Stone Age,* Charles Scribner's Sons, New York, third edition, 1925; Figs. 5–6 and pp. 115–214.

France[4]; or, in a cave on the coast of Italy, a man's skull surrounded (like some of the bear skulls) with a neat oval of stones, and with receptacles round about full of the bones of slaughtered beasts, indicating an offering and feast[5].

There can be no doubt that Neanderthal Man observed some sort of cult. Furthermore, the idea of a sanctuary is evident, within which a protective ritual was executed. And by analogy with all that we know of the religious activities of later man, this ceremonialism points to a sense of the holy: that peculiar sentiment which Rudolf Otto identified as the unique, distinctive category of religion. "That mental state", as Rudolf Otto has declared, "is perfectly *sui generis* and irreducible to any other.... While it admits of being discussed, it cannot be strictly defined.... It cannot, strictly speaking, be taught, it can only be evoked, awakened in the mind; as everything that comes 'of the spirit' must be awakened[6]."

We have to ask, therefore: What was the occasion, the empirical experience, that awakened in man (or even proto-man, if you like) that state of spiritual arrest before the numinous which has been cherished and cultivated ever since as the highest, deepest, and most luminous state of mind of which the human being is capable?

We do not know what death can have meant to the paleolithic hunter. Nevertheless, some sense of its force can be gained from certain primitive races living in the world today; for incredible though it may seem, the hunting cults of the paleolithic age survive among many of the tribes of northern Asia and America.

For example, among the Ainus of Japan there is still practiced a bear sacrifice that any visitor with a bit of luck can observe. The Ainu are a

---

[4] Ibid., pp. 221–22, citing H. KLAATSCH and O. HAUSER, *Homo aurignacensis Hauseri, ein paläolithischer Skelettfund aus dem unteren Aurignacien der Station Combe-Capelle bei Montferrand (Périgord)*, "Prähistorische Zeitschrift", Bd. I, 1909 (Heft 3–4, 1910), pp. 273–338.

[5] A. C. BLANC, *L'homme fossile du Mont Circé*, "L'Anthropologie", Tome 49, N° 3, Paris 1939, pp. 253–64.

[6] RUDOLF OTTO, *The Idea of the Holy*, translation by J. W. HARVEY, Oxford University Press, third impression, revised, 1925, p. 7.

puzzling race; for, although their neighbors are Mongolians for thousands of miles around, their skin is white and they have blue eyes, wavy hair, and immense beards. These interesting people have the wonderful idea that the world of men is so much more interesting and beautiful than that of the gods that deities like to come here and pay us visits. On all such occasions they are in disguise, wearing the bodies of animals, birds, fish, or insects. The bear is a visiting mountain god; the owl a village god; the dolphin a god of the sea. Trees, too, are gods on earth; and even the tools that men make become gods if properly wrought. Swords, for example, may be gods. But of all these, the most honored divine visitor is the bear[7].

There is a difficulty, however, that confronts the god on the occasion of his visit; for he cannot quit the animal form that he has assumed and return to his own home until the animal is killed: the god is locked, so to say, in its animal costume. And so the hunter, killing the animal, releases the god—and this, it is believed, is something the deity desires; for although he has come to us on a visit, he does not wish to remain here forever, as a dolphin, as an owl, or as a bear.

One can readily see that for any people whose whole mode of life is that of direct killing—dealing death, hand to hand—such a mythology would be of considerable psychological importance; for although, as Spengler has declared, "man is a beast of prey", man, like no other beast, knows what he is doing when he kills. Like no other beast of prey, he has the knowledge of death and knows, when he kills, that he is, indeed, killing. The first function of myth, therefore, as it would now appear, was to conquer death, that is to say, to overcome the psychological impact of the act and necessity of killing. "For it takes a powerful magic", as Leo Frobenius once remarked, "to spill blood and not be overtaken by the blood revenge[8]."

Or perhaps we can even go a step further and say that a certain hint of the Freudian Oedipus complex is here to be identified; for if it is true,

---

[7] Kyosuki Kindaiti, *Ainu Life and Legends,* Tourist Library 36, Tokyo 1941, p. 50.

[8] Leo Frobenius, "Atlantis", Vol. I, *Volksmärchen der Kabylen,* Eugen Diederichs, Jena 1921, p. 15.

as Géza Róheim has said, that *Father* is the first enemy and everything killed is therefore *Father,* then the fear of spilled blood and the compulsion to atone—to wipe out the death—is heavily charged, not only with noumenal, but also with Oedipal dread.

When a bear is killed by an Ainu hunter, the man comes running down from the mountain to his village, shouting that a god is about to pay the people a visit. A number of young men then join him and, in a kind of procession, they carry the dead bear into the man's house by way not of the door but of a hole knocked in the wall—the so-called "god's window". Such an entry is known as a "god's arrival". Furthermore, the fire burning in the center of the house, on the hearth, is a goddess—a mountain goddess, just as the bear is a mountain god; for in Japan volcanic fire is a well-known phenomenon. Fujiyama is an extinct volcano, and it surely is no accident that the Ainu name of their goddess Fire, protectress of the hearth, is Fuji. When the bear is carried in triumph to the house,the fire goddess bids him welcome. He enters by the "god's window" and the two, god and goddess, converse together by the fireside all night, while the people sing and play music to entertain them. The next day, when the bear is slaughtered, cooked, and eaten, offerings of its own meat are made to its head, which is placed in the seat of honor; and when the bear is supposed to have finished eating, the god is given thanks for his visit, praise and many presents, and, ceremonially dismissed, returns to his mountain home[9].

When a very young black bear is caught in the mountains it is carried back alive to the village with a great deal of shouting, as a divine little visitor. One of the women adopts it, takes it to nurse at her breast, lets it play about with her children and treats it with great affection. When it becomes big enough to hurt and scratch, however, it is put into a cage and kept there for about two years. Then comes the time when it is thought proper to release the young bear from its body and send it back to its divine home. This sacrifice is not regarded as a cruel act, but as one of kindness to the visitor. It is called *iyomande,* meaning "to send

---

[9] KINDAITI, op. cit., pp. 51–52.

away", and though a certain cruelty and baiting are involved, the bear is supposed to be extremely happy.

The man who is to give the feast calls out to the people of his village: "I am about to sacrifice the dear little divine thing from among the mountains. Come, my friends, to the feast. Let us enjoy together the pleasures of this 'sending away'!"

A number of prayer-sticks are made. These are called "message bearers". They are from two to five feet long, whittled in such a way as to leave shavings clustered at the top, and they are stuck into the earth, beside the hearth fire, where the fire goddess dwells, after which they are brought to the place where the bear is to be killed.

The men of the village now approach the cage; the women and children follow, dancing and singing. All sit in a circle before the bear, and the leader, sitting very close to the cage, lets the little visiting god know what is going to happen.

"O Divine One", he says to the cub, "you were sent into this world for us to hunt. Precious little divinity, we adore you; pray, hear our prayer. We have nourished and brought you up with a deal of pains and trouble, because we love you so. And now that you have grown big, we are about to send you back to your father and mother. When you come to them, please speak well of us and tell them how kind we have been. Please come to us again and we shall again do you the honor of a sacrifice."

Ladies and gentlemen, please observe: the bear is invited to return. "Come to us again, and we shall again do you the honor of a sacrifice." To these people of the North—these people of the bear sacrifice—there is no such thing as death. There is no such thing as a beginning in birth. For death and birth are simply the passing back and forth of an immortal individual through a veil or curtain. And the function of the rite is to facilitate and celebrate this passage. It is not the re-enactment, here and now, of an archetypal event that first took place in the beginning of time, *in illo tempore*. There is no such concept in this mythology. It is simply that the bear is now going home and should carry away no sentiment of ill will; and if it should wish to come again it may be sure that it will be honorably greeted, given a good home, and sent away with gifts.

The young bear, secured with ropes, is made to walk around the circle of the people. Blunt little arrows are shot at him and he is teased until he becomes furious. Then he is tied to a decorated stake; six young fellows seize him by the legs, the head and tail; two poles, called "poles for strangling", are held to his neck, above and below; a perfect bowman sends an arrow into his heart in such a way that no blood spills to the earth; the poles are squeezed together, and the little guest is gone.

The bear's head then is removed with the whole hide, feet and tail attached, carried into the house and arranged among prayer-sticks and valuable gifts, to share a parting feast. A tasty morsel of its own flesh is placed beneath its snout, along with a helping of dried fish, some millet dumplings, a cup of *sake* or beer, and a bowl of its own stew. Then it is honored with another speech:

"O Little Cub, we give you these prayer-sticks, dumplings, and dried fish; take them to your parents. Go straight to your parents without hanging about on your way, or some devils will snatch away the souvenirs. And when you arrive, say to your parents: 'I have been nourished for a long time by an Ainu father and mother and have been kept from all trouble and harm. Since I am now grown up, I have returned. And I have brought these prayer-sticks, cakes, and dried fish. Please rejoice!' If you say this to them, Little Cub, they will be very happy."

A feast is celebrated, there is dancing, more prayer-sticks are made and placed upon the bear's head, another bowl of its own stew is placed before it, and when time has been allowed for it to finish, the man presiding at the feast calls out: "The little god is finished; come, let us worship!" He takes the bowl, salutes it, and divides the contents among the guests. The other parts of the beast then are eaten also, while some of the men drink the blood for strength and smear a portion upon their clothes. The head of the bear is separated from the rest of the skin and, being set upon a pole called "the pole for sending away", it is placed among a number of other skulls remaining from earlier feasts. And for the next few days the festival continues, until every bit of the little god has been consumed[10].

"It is perfectly evident", writes Dr. Herbert Kühn in comment upon these rites and others of their kind, "that the usages and customs of the Interglacial period have been retained up to the very present in these peripheral regions of the earth. . . . The bear skulls still are flayed and preserved in sacred places, offering places. They are covered and set round with slabs of stone. Special ceremonies still are celebrated at the offering places. Even today two vertebrae of the neck are allowed to remain attached to the skull, just as then. And even today we often find that the large molar of the bear has been ground down, precisely as Luther Friedrich Zotz found the case to be in the course of an excavation of a series of caves in the glacial mountain heights of Silesia[11]."

"Such details among the contemporary Asiatic hunters as the grinding down of the tooth of the bear and leaving of two vertebrae attached to the skull, just as in the European Interglacial period, prove that the continuity has actually remained unbroken for tens of thousands of years[12]."

It is to be noted, also, that in the Alpine caves remains were found of fire. But Neanderthal Man did not cook his food. Is it then possible that fire was first domesticated, not for any practical use but as a fetish: as the living presence of that mountain goddess whom we have just beheld in conversation with the bear? She is a deity of considerable importance among the Ainu, serving not only as a guardian mother of the house, but also as a guide of souls to the other world.

And so let us attend, now, an Ainu funeral, noting its resemblance

---

[10] I. BACHELOR, article "Ainus", *Encyclopedia of Religion and Ethics* (ed. James Hastings), Charles Scribner's Sons, New York 1928, Vol. I, pp. 249–50, and KINDAITI, op. cit., pp. 52–54.

[11] LUTHER FRIEDRICH ZOTZ, *Die schlesischen Höhlen und ihre eiszeitlichen Bewohner*, Breslau 1937; *Die Altsteinzeit in Niederschlesien*, Leipzig 1939. Also, WILHELM KOPPERS, *Künstlicher Zahnschliff am Bären im Altpaläolithikum und bei den Ainu auf Sachalin*, "Quartar", 1938, pp. 97 ff.

[12] HERBERT KÜHN, *Das Problem des Urmonotheismus*, "Abhandlungen der Geistes- und Sozialwissenschaftlichen Klasse", Akademie der Wissenschaften und der Literatur in Mainz, Jahrgang 1950, Nr. 22, Franz-Steiner-Verlag, Wiesbaden.

to the "sending away" of the bear and then recalling the matter of those two Neanderthal graves.

Among the Ainu, on such an occasion the master of the family becomes the celebrant. "You are a god now", he says to the corpse. "And without hankering for this world, you are to go now to the world of the gods, where your ancestors abide. They will thank you for the presents that you bring. So now, go on quickly! Do not pause to look back." He puts a pair of leggings on the voyager's legs, a pair of mittens on his hands. "Take care", he tells him, "not to lose your way. The old goddess of the fire will guide you aright. I have already asked her to do so. Rely on her, and go your way with care. Farewell!"

A rich dinner is prepared for both the spirit of the departed and the people at the wake; and when they are about to carry away the coffin, the celebrant again has a word for their departing friend. "We have made a fine staff to help you on your way. Take hold of it firmly at the top and walk securely, minding your feet, lifting and lowering them as you raise and lower the staff. You have plenty of food and drink as souvenirs. Look neither to right nor to left but go on quickly and delight your ancestors with your presents. Forget your brothers, sisters, and other relatives remaining in this world. They are safe and sound under the care of the old goddess Fire. Do not brood upon them or else the folks where you are going will laugh at you."

The coffin is not carried out through the door, but a part of the side of the house is taken away and repaired before the mourners return. The ghost, then, will not know how to get back in. Or if the one who has died is the mistress of the house, the whole dwelling is burned. Into the grave go jewels, ear-rings, kitchen knives, pots and ladles, looms and other such, if the departed was a woman; swords, bows, and quivers, if a man. And when the burial, or "throwing away" as it is called, has been completed, the mourners leave the grave walking backward, lest turning they should be possessed by the ghost of the deceased; and they are holding weapons in their hands—the women sticks, the men their swords—which they wave back and forth for their defense[13].

---

[13] KINDAITI, op. cit., pp. 41–47.

The sentiment or experience illustrated by this rite is precisely that which Rudolf Otto has termed "daemonic dread". As he declares, this is not equivalent to any natural fear. No natural fear passes over into it merely by being intensified. It is the first, crude, primitive form of the numinous dread of the higher mystical experience[14].

But in these rites the obvious intention is to ban or block the impact of this dread. A myth has been invented—the myth of no death—to protect the mind from the necessity of adjusting itself to an invasion from that abyss of darkness over which all life rides. "Life", wrote Schopenhauer, "is something that should not have been." The plants do not know this. The animals do not know this. For, as Dr. Neumann observed in his eloquent lecture the first day of this "Tagung", the animals are rooted in nature. They play their natural roles without anxiety, like the sun, like the moon, like the stars. Man, however, has become alienated from his source and experiences nature with dread, both in its macrocosmic aspect, as the objective world over against which his consciousness stands as subject, and in its microcosmic aspect, as the spontaneity of his own nature—his unconscious, his joy in being.

The hunter, daily dealing death, is washed in blood—as, indeed, is all of nature. And the first myth of the self-protective ego, defending itself from the necessity of yielding its own blood to be the life of the world, is that of an immortal ground underlying the phenomenology of the passing world.

This comforting myth, this protective idea that there is no such thing as death but only a going away and in birth only a returning, this idea that fundamentally nothing happens but all is a mere appearance, disappearance and reappearance—a sort of cosmic peek-a-boo game—is one that occurs spontaneously to children. Jean Piaget, in his volume on *The Child's Conception of the World*, presents a number of examples of the infant's thoughts in this regard:

"Do people turn back into babies when they get very old?" asked a little fellow, five years of age.

---

[14] OTTO, op. cit., pp. 16–17.

"When you die", asked another, "do you grow up again?"

"And then", said the child of Dr. Melanie Klein, "I'll die, and you too, Mamma, and then we'll come back again[15]."

Such infantile ideas cannot properly be called myths, but they are the elements, the bricks, so to say, out of which mythologies are made.

There is a legend of the Blackfoot Indians of the North American plains that reveals the force of these defensive ideas, not only for the psychological protection of the beast of prey that knows what he is doing when he kills, but also for the moral organization of his community. The Blackfoot Indians of Montana were buffalo hunters and one of their best devices for slaughtering a large herd was to lure the animals over a cliff and butcher them when they fell on the rocks below.

Now the legend of which I speak tells of a time when the hunters, for some reason, could not induce the animals to the fall, so that the people were starving. And so one early morning, when a young woman went to get water and saw a herd of buffalo feeding on the prairie, right at the edge of the cliff above the fall, she cried out: "Oh! if you will only jump into the corral, I shall marry one of you." She was amazed when the animals began to come jumping, falling over the cliff; but when a big bull with a single bound cleared the walls of the corral and approached her, she was terrified.

"Come!" he said, and he took her arm.

"Oh no!" she cried, pulling back.

"But you said that if the buffalo would jump, you would marry one. See! The corral is filled." And without further ado, he led her away onto the prairie.

Now when the people missed the young woman, her father took his bow and set out to find her. Arriving at a buffalo wallow—a place where the buffalo come for water and to lie and roll—he sat down to consider what he should do, and while he was brooding, a beautiful black and white bird, a magpie, came and lighted on the ground.

"Ha!" said the man. "You are a handsome bird! Help me! As you

---

[15] JEAN PIAGET, *The Child's Conception of the World*, Harcourt, Brace and Company, New York 1929, p. 362.

fly about, look for my daughter, and if you see her, say: 'Your father is waiting by the wallow!'"

The bird flew to a nearby herd and, seeing a young woman among the bison, lit on the ground not far from her and said quietly: "Your father is waiting by the wallow!"

"Not so loud!" she whispered, frightened, looking around; for her bull husband was sleeping close by. "Go back and tell him to wait."

When the bull woke, he said to his wife: "Go get me some water."

So she took a horn from his head and hurried to the wallow. "Father!" she cried, "Why did you come? You will surely be killed." And when he urged her to run with him, she refused. "They would pursue and kill us", she said. "We must wait until he sleeps again."

She returned, and the bull drank a swallow from his horn. "Aha!" said he. "There is a person close by."

"No! No!" she answered.

The bull drank some more; then got up and bellowed. What a terrible sound! Up stood the bulls, raised their short tails and shook them, tossed their great heads, and bellowed back. Then they rushed in all directions and, coming to the wallow, hooked the poor man with their horns and trampled him, so that soon not even a small piece of his body could be seen.

Then his daughter cried. "Oh, my father, my father!"

"Ah-ha!" said the bull. "You are mourning for your father. And so now, perhaps, you can see how it is with us. We have seen our mothers, fathers, many of our relatives, hurled over the rock walls and slaughtered by your people. But I shall pity you. If you can bring your father to life again, you and he may go back to your people."

The woman turned to the magpie. "Help me!" she said. "Go and search in the trampled mud. Try to find some little piece of my father's body."

The bird quickly flew, tore up the mud with his sharp beak, and then, at last, found something white: a joint of the backbone. The young woman placed this particle on the ground and, covering it with her robe, sang a certain song. Removing the robe, she saw her father's body lying there, as though dead. Covering it again, she resumed her song, and when she next took the robe away, her father was breathing; then he stood up. The buffalo were amazed.

"We have seen strange things today", the bull husband said to the others. "The man we trampled into small pieces is alive again. The people's holy power is strong."

He turned to the young woman. "Now", he said, "before you and your father go, we shall teach you our dance and song. You must not forget them."

For this ritual of the buffalo dance was to be the magical means by which the buffalo killed by the people for their food should be restored to life, just as the man killed by the buffalo had been restored.

All the buffalo danced; and as befitted the dance of such great beasts, the song was slow and solemn, the step ponderous and deliberate. And when the dance was over, the bull said: "Now go to your home and do not forget what you have seen. Teach this dance and song to your people. The sacred object of the rite is to be a bull's head and buffalo robe. Likewise all those who dance the bulls are to wear a bull's head and buffalo robe when they perform."

The father and daughter returned to their camp and the chiefs selected a number of young men, who were taught the dance and song of the bulls. That was the way the Blackfoot association of men's societies called All Comrades first was organized. Its function was to regulate the ceremonial life and to punish offenders[16].

One finds a great many tales of this sort among the North American tribes. Their basic point is that there is a mutual understanding between the human and animal worlds, according to which the game animals give their bodies willingly to be man's food. The animals are willing victims. But there is an understanding, also, that the hunters will perform a ritual of renewal, so that the herds may be restored to life. The resurrection of the dead man was made possible by the finding of a particle of bone. Without this, nothing could have been accomplished, but with it, he

---

[16] GEORGE BIRD GRINNELL, *Blackfoot Lodge Tales,* Charles Scribner's Sons, New York 1916, pp. 104–7; 220–24.

returned just as he had been before. We may regard this bone as our token of the hunter's nuclear idea of the miracle of renewal. The bone does not disintegrate in the womb of the earth and germinate into something else, like a planted seed, but is the undestroyed base from which the same individual that was there before becomes magically reconstructed, to pick up life where he left it. The same creature comes back by way of an actual fragment or element of his former body.

Furthermore, this rite was in no sense a re-enactment of any archetypal event from the "time of the beginning". The rites of the primitive hunters are not supposed to have descended from an age of mythological ancestors. They are said to have come, for the most part, directly from the animals themselves—from just such Animal Masters, or Master Animals, as the buffalo bull of this legend. And they have been received by such people as dwell in the world today, possessed however of shaman power. The atmosphere of this mythology is not mystical, but magical and shamanistic. The girl, even without knowing it, had shaman power; the great bull, too, had shaman power: he jumped and was not killed like the rest; the magpie was a shaman. According to the view of these people such power exists among shamans and visionaries to this day and it is through them—not from the ancestors of a mythological age— that the people have received their rites.

One more aspect of these shamanistic, hunting mythologies and rites must now be shown, namely the cosmology underlying them; and in order to suggest something of the broad geographical range of this primitive mode of thought, I shall choose my illustration from an African tribe. Many of the African tribes are planters. The pigmies, however, have an ancient tradition of the hunt; and so, when four of these little people—a woman and three men—attached themselves to an expedition conducted by Leo Frobenius in the Congo, he one day asked them if they would supply the company with some antelope meat. They replied that they would have to wait until the next day, because there were some preparations to be made that could be accomplished only at dawn, and Frobenius then kept his eye on them to see what these preparations might be.

Before sunrise the four little people climbed a nearby hill and, when they had reached the summit, cleared the ground of all bits of growth. One of the men then drew something on the cleared earth while the others pronounced formulae and prayers. As soon as the sun appeared, one of the men, with an arrow in his drawn bow, stepped over to the cleared ground and, when the rays of the sun struck the drawing, the following ritual took place. The woman, lifting her hands as though reaching for the sun, uttered loudly some unintelligible syllables, the man released his arrow, the woman cried again, and the men then dashed into the forest with their weapons. When Frobenius went to see what had been drawn, he found the outline of an antelope with the arrow in its neck.

That afternoon the hunters shot their quarry with an arrow through its neck. And they took from it some hair and a calabash of blood which they carried the next morning to the top of their hill for the second portion of the rite. The hairs and blood they smeared upon the picture and when the sun's rays again struck it, they quickly erased the whole thing and pulled out the arrow[17].

The crucial point of the ceremony was that the rite should be executed at dawn, the arrow flying into the antelope along the first ray of the sun. For in all hunting mythologies the sun is a great hunter. At dawn his arrows slay the stars. By analogy: the human hunter is to be identified with the sun, his arrow with a ray of the sun, the antelope with a star. Then, just as tomorrow night will see the star return, so will tomorrow the antelope. And the woman, apparently, was the cosmic night itself: the womb of renewal and gate of return.

In the celebrated Cro-Magnon painted grotto of Altamira, which is to be dated approximately from 35,000 to 10,000 B.C., we find the same idea illustrated. For those beautiful bulls, so often reproduced, are painted on the ceiling. They are stars. The cave is the cosmic night and they are the shining, immortal herd of the night sky—the archetypes of those annual herds that appear, as willing victims, to give their bodies and return.

---

[17] LEO FROBENIUS, *Das unbekannte Afrika,* Oskar Beck, München 1923, pp. 34–35.

"On earth, as it is in heaven": that is the theme. Man is returned to the innocence of the sun and stars, and of the animal world, which is rooted in nature, by an equation of himself with the sun, the great lion of the heavens, and of his victims with the herds of the night sky. And by concentrating on these, he is able to erase from consciousness the actual threat of the night of annihilation. The reality of nature and himself as nature has been countered by a myth of personal immortality.

"After death", said an Eskimo shaman, Igjugarjuk by name, whom the explorer, Dr. Rasmussen, met in the arctic of northern Canada, "we do not always remain as we were during life. The souls of men, for instance, may turn into all kinds of animals. Pinga, the guardian spirit of the universe, looks after the souls of animals and does not like to see too many of them killed. Nothing is lost. The blood and entrails must be covered up after a caribou has been killed. So we see that life is endless. Only we do not know in what form we shall reappear[18]."

The rites and myths are childish—as, indeed, all rituals are and all mythologies. The inhabiting idea, however, of the Self transcending death is one that we know from the greatest teachers of mankind: the Lord Krishna's song, for example, or the sages of the Greeks.

"Know that by which all of this is pervaded to be imperishable", we read in the *Bhagavad Gītā*. "Only the bodies, of which this eternal, imperishable, incomprehensible Self is the indweller, can be said to have an end[19]."

And from the Greek sage, Pythagoras:

"All things are changing; nothing dies. The spirit wanders, comes now here, now there, and occupies whatever frame it pleases. From beasts it passes into human bodies, and from our bodies into beasts, but never perishes[20]."

This I would like to call the primary myth of the masculine spirit, summoned into manifestation by the challenge of death: the abyss of

---

[18] KNUD RASMUSSEN, *Across Arctic America,* G. P. Putnam's Sons, New York and London 1927, p. 80.
[19] *Bhagavad Gītā* 2:17–18.
[20] OVID, *Metamorphoses,* XV, 165–68.

the deep night sky, both without and within: the night of being and becoming absolutely nothing.

And I should like to pose, now, in contrast to this, the contrary myth that appears in those parts of our planet in which the plant world, and not the animal, is the dominant factor and determinant of human experience. There the primary symbol, the archetype of experience, is not the bone, which does not dissolve in the earth, but the seed, which indeed does so: dies, so to say, and in death is transformed into something other, which then is the nourishment and very substance of all life. And here, furthermore, it is not upon the work and life feeling of the male that the community depends, but upon the female, who, in her normal functioning as mother and nourisher, participates in the nature of the bearing earth itself and deeply knows, therefore, its secret.

Leo Frobenius was the first to point out the contrast of these two mythological worlds, respectively, of the animal-taught and the plant-taught primitive societies. And it was just ten years ago that Professor Adolf Jensen, Director of the Institute for Culture Morphology in Frankfort, presented in this hall an example of the myth that I wish to bring before you as typical of the latter. We do not know how far back in time these planting myths are to be traced. They are of far more recent origin than those of the Animal Master and the Bear Sacrifice. And yet, their great age is well attested by their prodigious distribution: from the jungles of West Africa eastward to India and Southeast Asia, across the Pacific to equatorial America. Their field, in fact, is that whole vast equatorial belt, where the primary source of man's food is not the hunt, but the cultivation of such nourishing fare as the banana, coconut, breadfruit, and yam. And among the characteristic traits of this zone there is a basic, widely diffused myth that represents our present world of death and birth as having come into being only following an act of murder.

In the beginning, we are told, there was no death; there was no begetting of new beings; and there were no food plants, for there was no need to eat; there was no moon to mark the passages of time; and there was no division of creatures into men and beasts. Nor were the people of that mythological age precisely people: they partook of animal and plant as well as human traits.

According to an Indonesian version of this general myth, the nine first families of mankind emerged from clusters of bananas, and where they settled there were nine dance grounds. A certain man among them, however, killed a pig, and this was the first killing of anything in the world. He found a coconut on the tusk of this pig: the first coconut in the world; and when he planted it—having wrapped it, first, in a piece of cloth bearing the picture of a serpent—a palm tree grew. The man climbed this palm to cut from it a blossom, but cut his own hand while doing so, and from the mixture of blood and palm sap a little girl was born, whom he called Hainuwele, "Leaf of the Cocopalm". She grew very fast and in three days was mature. Then a great dance that was to last nine nights was celebrated on the nine dance grounds. The men danced in a large ninefold spiral and the women sat in the center, reaching betel nut to the dancers, just as they do in the festivals to this day. Hainuwele stood in the center; but instead of passing out betel nut, she gave the men all kinds of wonderful things, valuable objects that had come from her body, such as coral, beautiful dishes, golden ear-rings, and great gongs. The people pressed about her for more, but presently became jealous of her wealth. And so the men dug a deep hole in the dance area and, while she was passing out these objects, in the course of their slowly cycling movement they pressed her toward the hole and threw her in. A loud song drowned her cry. They quickly covered her with dirt and the dancers trampled this with their steps, dancing till dawn, when the festival ended.

But when Hainuwele failed to come home her father knew that she had been killed. He went to the dance ground, dug up the corpse, cut it into many pieces, and buried these in the area round about. Then the buried portions of the body began to grow, turning into things that up to that time had never existed anywhere on earth, the plants that have been the food of the people ever since.

Thus death came into the world and with it the food by which men live. The world lives on death: that is the insight rendered in this myth.

Moreover, as we learn from other mythological fragments in this culture sphere, the sexual organs appeared at that time; for death without reproduction would have been the end, as, likewise, reproduction without death.

We may say, then, that the interdependence of *thanatos* and *eros*, their import as the complementary aspects of a single state of being, and the necessity of killing—killing and eating—for the continuance of this state of being, which is that of man on earth, and of all things on earth, the animals, birds, and fish, as well as man—this deeply moving, emotionally disturbing glimpse of death as the life of the living—is the fundamental motivation supporting the rites around which the social structure of the early planting villages was composed. They place death in the middle of the scene: and not death alone, but killing—as the precondition of life.

The headhunt is practiced in this culture zone as a ritual act preliminary to marriage; for as murder preceded begetting *in illo tempore,* so must it now. Here killing is not an act of heroism, but of religion, rendering here and now the monstrous archetype, so that life may realize the awful depth of its own nature—not with dread, but with surrender[21].

A typical ritual of this zone has been described by the Swiss ethnologist Paul Wirz, in his work on the Marind-anim of Dutch South New Guinea. The mythological beings of the age of the beginning appear in the ceremonies of these headhunting cannibals to enact the world-fashioning events of the mythological age to the tireless chant of many voices, the boom of log drums, and the whirring of the bull-roarers, which are the voices of the mythological beings themselves, rising from the earth. Toward the end of the boys' puberty rites, which terminate in a sexual orgy of several days and nights, from which, however, the boys themselves are excluded, a fine young girl, ceremonially painted and costumed, is led into the dancing ground and made to lie beneath a

---

[21] ADOLF E. JENSEN, *Die mythische Weltbetrachtung der alten Pflanzer-Völker,* "Eranos-Jahrbuch" XVII/1949, Rhein-Verlag, Zürich 1950; also, ibid., *Das religiöse Weltbild einer frühen Kultur,* August-Schröder-Verlag, Stuttgart 1949.

platform of very heavy logs. With her, in open view of the festival, the initiates then cohabit, one after another; and while the youth chosen to be last is embracing her, the supports of the logs are jerked away and the platform drops to a great boom of drums: a howl goes up and the dead girl and boy are dragged from the logs, cut up, roasted, and eaten[22].

This savage ritual is typical of the culture world of the Great Goddess, who is at once the womb and tomb of the universe. And even where the victims are not boys and girls but animals—pigs, for example, goats, or bulls—the victim is never an offering in the sense of a gift rendered to some god, but is the god itself. Its death is a rendering here and now of the mystery of that one who becomes many in us all by way of a continuous immolation. This divinity is androgyne, as well as both dead and begetting at the same time.

Nor is it possible to miss the echo of this solemn goat-song in the myths and rites of the early agricultural civilizations: the mythologies of Ishtar and Tammuz, Isis and Osiris. In the earliest civilizations of the archaic world the evidence for rites involving the immolation, not simply of such a young couple, but of the entire royal court, is overwhelming.

In the Royal Tombs of the ancient Sumerian city of Ur, Sir Leonard Woolley excavated a number of spectacular group burials. In one he found the chamber of a king and beside it that of his queen (or perhaps these two, as later students have observed, may have been a substituted priest and priestess; for their date, c. 2500 B.C., is a little late for this sort of royal immolation[23]). The members of the king's court had been disposed around his tomb in perfect order; and above these, likewise in perfect order, were the skeletons of the queen's court, which, apparently, had followed. The queen herself had been dressed precisely in the manner in which the goddess Ishtar is described in the Mesopotamian myths of her voluntary descent to the underworld following her spouse,

---

[22] PAUL WIRZ, *Die Marind-anim von Holländisch-Süd-Neuguinea*, L. Friedrichsen and Co., Hamburg, Vol. II, 1925, pp. 40–44.

[23] Cf. HENRI FRANKFORT, *Kingship and the Gods: A Study of Ancient Near Eastern Religion as the Integration of Society and Nature*, University of Chicago Press, Chicago 1948, pp. 400–401, note 12.

and at the queen's hand there was a golden cup, which had contained her drink of death. Among the rich ornaments in her chamber there lay the silver head of a cow: in the king's chamber, the head of a bull. And there were a number of beautiful little harps among the remains, one still caressed by the skeleton hand of its girl harpist, the sounding box having the form of a bull, with a bull's head of gold, embellished with a lapis lazuli beard[24].

We know this bull from the myths. It is the moon-bull, Sin, who dies and is resurrected, and the rhythm of whose cycle is the rhythm of the womb.

Hainuwele, the Indonesian sacrifice, not only became the plant world upon which mankind lives, but also, after three days, rose into the sky as the moon. Her animal counterpart, furthermore, was the pig, as the king's, here, is the bull. Her murder followed that of the pig and just as the coconut from which she grew was derived from the pig's death, so were the other plants from hers. Many other mythologies of this planting-culture zone assign the first death to a man-serpent—a sort of *nāga*—whose head then was cut off and planted: and this would seem to have been the earliest pattern of the myth. A vestige appears in the tale of Hainuwele in the serpent painted on the cloth in which the coconut was wrapped before planting. For the growth, then, of the coconut tree, as the first valuable food plant, reproduced in every nut the form of the man-serpent's head. And the headhunt, also, is now well explained as a ritual repetition of that decapitation: particularly, since the head is to be opened in a certain way, like a coconut, and the contents consumed.

Another vestige of the serpent as the first sacrifice appears in our own serpent, winding up the tree, addressing Eve in conversation[25]. Eve and the serpent are the archetypal couple through whom death and birth came into the world. They were not murdered during, but cursed following, their mythological act and we have instead of the coconut an apple; nevertheless, all the elements of the primitive planting myth are present.

---

[24] Sir LEONARD WOOLLEY, *Ur of the Chaldees,* Ernest Benn, Ltd., London 1929, pp. 46–56.
[25] *Genesis* 3.

In the mythology of the primitive planters, death and renewal are not pictured as a curse, but as a monstrous wonder, wherein the divine being whose flesh is meat indeed and whose blood is drink indeed becomes our very flesh and we, in turn, then yield our own flesh in reenactment. The cross of Christ, rising on Calvary, "The Hill of the Skull", Golgotha, where Adam's head is supposed to have been buried, supports and validates our own creative civilization with the force of this terrible image. Growing from the buried head of the First Adam, like a tree, bearing on its boughs the Second Adam, "Fruit of the Tree", Holy Rood has made of man's death the sign of man's rebirth: and it surely is in the spirit of that willing sacrifice that both the Royal Tombs of Ur and the primitive rituals of the early planters must be viewed.

An early Portuguese voyager in South India tells of a certain king whom he saw in Malabar (which to this day is an area with a very strong matriarchal emphasis), who, on a certain day determined by the position of the planet Jupiter in the zodiac, mounted a platform before his people and with some very sharp knives cut off his nose, ears, lips, and other members, and as much of himself as he could, throwing everything away hurriedly until so much of his blood was gone that he began to faint, whereupon he quickly cut his throat[26].

Or consider the largest of the Royal Tombs of Ur, where the remains of sixty-eight women were found in regular rows, each lying on her side, legs slightly bent and hands brought up to her face, so close together that the heads of those in front rested on the legs of those behind. Twenty-eight had worn hair ribbons of gold, all but one of the rest, hair ribbons of silver; and there were four harpists grouped together about a copper cauldron, which Woolley associates with the manner of their death—a poison, voluntarily drunk, which had carried this multitude through the winged gate. They had met their death in the way of a great game; for all were stars. Their king was the moon: his queen was Ishtar,

---

[26] DUARTE BARBOSA, *A Description of the Coasts of East Africa and Malabar in the Sixteenth Century,* Hakluyt Society, London 1866, p. 172; cited by Sir JAMES G. FRAZER, *The Golden Bough,* one-volume edition, The Macmillan Company, New York 1922, pp. 274–75.

the planet Venus. An eon had ended, and the whole celestial court dissolved into the night, as prerequisite to renewal: renewal, however, not of the individuals, but of the game—the civilization. For in this tradition there was no such thing, really, as an individual in our sense. All were but organs of the group. And with an attitude of acquiescence in the process, submission, or even—I might say—*amor fati,* their bodies were given to the earth, like seeds, for the renewal and continuous re-creation of the world.

And what of that one young lady who had no ribbon, either of gold or of silver? Actually, she had a ribbon of silver on her person. It was found among the bones of her skeleton at the level of the waist: carried apparently in her pocket, just as she had taken it from her room, done up in a tight coil with the ends brought over to prevent its coming undone. She had been late for the party and had not had time to put it on[27].

The contrast between these planters' myths and rites and those of the hunters, I should say, could not be greater. They represent the two elementary poles of response to the *mysterium tremendum:* that of defense and that of surrender. And whereas there is something charmingly boyish about the first, in the second the whole mystery of woman's range of life experience comes into play: the way of experience tellingly rendered in the words of a noble Abyssinian woman quoted by Frobenius in one of his African studies.

"How", this woman asked, "can a man know what a woman's life is? A woman's life is quite different from a man's. God has ordered it so. A man is the same from the time of his circumcision to the time of his withering. He is the same before he has sought out a woman for the first time, and afterwards. But the day when a woman enjoys her first love cuts her in two. She becomes another woman on that day. The man is the same after his first love as he was before. The woman is from the day of her first love another. That continues so all through life. The man spends a night by a woman and goes away. His life and body are always

---

[27] WOOLLEY, loc. cit.

the same. The woman conceives. As a mother she is another person than the woman without child. She carries the fruit of the night nine months long in her body. Something grows. Something grows into her life that never again departs from it. She is a mother. She is and remains a mother even though her child die, though all her children die. For at one time she carried the child under her heart. And it does not go out of her heart ever again. Not even when it is dead. All this a man does not know; he knows nothing[28]."

The point is that woman is life, and goes with it in her experience; that life is what there is to know, and its nature is transformation.

With this then as our clue to the feminine mystique of the goddess Earth and her child, the plant child who is to be consumed, let us ask now, in conclusion, to what deepest depth of prehistory the earlier, hunter's way of thought can be traced. I have said that the Alpine cave-bear sanctuaries and human burials of Neanderthal Man represent the earliest *unquestionable* evidence of mythology and ritual. Some further clues, however, have recently appeared, which suggest an even greater depth than the Riss-Würm interglacial.

You have all heard of the bones recently unearthed in South Africa of a series of ape-like creatures, with the brain capacity about of a chimpanzee, but with upright posture. Their date is at the beginning of the Pleistocene: conservatively, about 600,000 B.C. And they have been named both Australopithecus ("the southern ape") and Plesianthropus ("proximate man"); for the question of their humanity is still under debate.

At the Fifth International Congress of Anthropological and Ethnological Sciences, held at the University of Pennsylvania in September 1956, Dr. Raymond Dart, of Witwatersrand University, South Africa, showed a convincing series of slides in which the bone implements of these creatures were illustrated. They included the lower jaws of large antelopes, which had been cut in half to be used as saws and knives;

---

[28] LEO FROBENIUS, *Der Kopf als Schicksal*, München 1924, p. 88, as cited by CARL KERÉNYI: C. G. JUNG and C. KERÉNYI, *Essays on a Science of Mythology*, Bollingen Series XXII, "Pantheon Books", New York 1949, pp. 141–42.

gazelle horns with part of the skull attached, which showed distinct signs of wear and use, possibly as digging tools; and a great number of Plesianthropoid palates with the teeth worn down, which had been used as scrapers. But the really sensational slides were those showing a number of baboon and Plesianthropoid skulls that had been fractured by the blow of a bludgeon. All had been struck by an instrument having two nubs or processes at the hitting end, which Professor Dart and his collaborators have surmised to have been the heavy end of the leg bone of a gazelle. But apes do not slay with weapons. Ergo: our little friend was not an ape, but a man[29].

The animal remains associated with the bones of these earliest known hominids have been chiefly antelopes, horses, gazelles, hyenas, giraffes and other beasts of the plains—very swift runners, so that the art of the hunt must have been considerably developed. Professor Dart, furthermore, has found abundant evidence of a practice of removing the heads and tails of the animals killed. From a sorting of about 6 tons of bone-bearing rock, representing the parts of at least 433 creatures, it was learned that Plesianthropus habitually decapitated the animals that he slew. The head parts of antelopes, the wild horse and ox, baboons, pigs, hyenas and porcupines, giraffes and rhinoceroses were found in great number, far separated from the bodies—and Professor Dart, in a recent paper on this subject, has compared this evidence of a head-cult with the cave-bear skulls of the Alpine sanctuaries—some 400,000 years later in date[30].

Throughout the length of this immense period there is no evidence of any kind suggesting a planter's cult or culture; and so it appears—at least from the evidence now available—that man was a killer from the start, a beast of prey, who knew, however, what he was doing when he killed and sought to protect himself by magic from its effect.

---

[29] RAYMOND DART, *Some Aspects of the Significance of the Australopithecine Osteodontokeratic Culture*, Vth International Congress of Anthropological and Ethnological Sciences, Philadelphia, September, 1956.

[30] RAYMOND DART, *The Makapansgat Australopithecine Osteodontokeratic Culture*, Third Panafrican Congress of Prehistory (ed. J. DESMOND CLARK), Chatto & Windus, London 1957, pp. 161-71.

II.

If an authority on architecture looking at the buildings of New York were to observe: "They are all made of brick"; then viewing the ruins of ancient Mesopotamia remarked: "They are all made of brick"; and finally, visiting the temples of Ceylon, declared: "They are all made of brick"; would you say that this man had an eye for the qualities of architecture? It is true that they are all of brick. It is true, also, that a study might be made of the differences between the bricks of Ceylon, those of ancient Sumer, those, say, of the Roman aqueducts still standing in southern France, and those of the city of New York. However, these observations about brick are not all that we should like to hear about the architecture of the great cities of the world.

Now let me present to you a problem in the architecture of myth.

Early one morning, long ago, two Sioux Indians on the North American plains were out hunting with their bows and arrows; and as they were standing on a hill looking for game, they saw in the distance something coming toward them in a very strange and wonderful manner. When this mysterious thing drew nearer, they perceived that it was a very beautiful woman, dressed in white buckskin and bearing a bundle on her back. One of the men immediately became lustful and told his friend of his desire, but the other rebuked him, warning that this surely was no ordinary woman. She had come close now and, setting down her bundle, asked the first to approach her. When he did so, he and she were suddenly covered by a cloud and when this lifted there was only the woman—with the man, nothing but bones at her feet, being consumed by snakes.

"Behold what you see!" she said to the other. "Now go and tell your people to prepare a large ceremonial lodge for my coming. I wish to announce to them something of great importance."

The young man returned quickly to this camp; and the chief, whose name was Standing Hollow Horn, had several teepees taken down, sewn together, and made into a ceremonial lodge. Such a lodge has twenty-eight poles, of which the central pole, the main support, is compared to the Great Spirit, Wakan Tanka, the supporter of the universe. The others represent aspects of creation; for the lodge itself is a likeness of the universe.

"If you add four sevens", said the old warrior priest, Black Elk, from whom this legend was derived, "you get twenty-eight. The moon lives twenty-eight days and we reckon time by the moon. Each day of the lunar month represents something sacred to our people: two of the days represent the Great Spirit, Wakan Tanka, who is our Father and Grandfather; two, the Earth, our Mother and Grandmother; four are for the four winds; one is for the spotted eagle; one for the sun, one for the moon, one for the morning star; four are for the four ages; seven for our seven great rites; one is for the buffalo; one for the fire; one for the water; one for the rock; and one is for man. You should know also that the buffalo has twenty-eight ribs, and that in our war bonnets we usually wear twenty-eight feathers. There is a meaning in everything, and these are the things that are good for men to know and to remember[31]."

The priest explained the image of the man consumed by snakes. "Anyone attached to the senses and things of this world", he said, "lives in ignorance and is being consumed by the snakes that represent his own passions[32]."

Are we not reminded here of the Greek myth of the young hunter, Actaeon, who, following a forest stream to its source, discovered the goddess Artemis, bathing in a pool, perfectly naked? And when she saw that he looked lustfully upon her, she turned him into a stag that was pursued by his own hounds, torn to pieces and consumed. The two myths are comparable. Black Elk's reading of his own accords with the sense of the Greek also. The two, that is to say, are made of bricks of the same kind.

But do such images take form naturally in the psyche? Can they be expected to appear any place on earth, spontaneously, in mythological systems? Or must we say, on the contrary, that since mythologies serve

---

[31] JOSEPH EPES BROWN, *The Sacred Pipe: Black Elk's Account of The Seven Rites of the Oglala Sioux*, University of Oklahoma Press, Norman, Oklahoma, 1953, p. 80.
[32] Ibid., p. 4, note 2.

specific, historically conditioned cultural functions—just as architectural structures do—if two can be shown to be homologous they are historically related? Can the Greeks and the Sioux possibly have received their inheritances from the same source? And are these common themes, therefore, evidence rather of cultural diffusion than of psychological spontaneity and parallel development? Before such questions can be answered, we must know more about the deities involved and their background. Let us continue, therefore, with this legend.

When the people had built a lodge that was symbolically a counterpart of the universe, they gathered within it and were extremely excited, wondering who the mysterious woman might be and what she wished to say. She entered by the door, which was facing east, and walked sunwise around the central pillar: south, west, north, and east. "For is not the south the source of life?" the old teller of the tale explained. "And does not man advance from there toward the setting sun of his life? Does he not then arrive, if he lives, at the source of light and understanding, which is the east? And does he not return to where he began, to his second childhood, there to give back his life to all life, and his flesh to the earth whence it came? The more you think about this", the old Indian said, "the more meaning you will see in it[33]."

Once again, we find that we are on familiar ground. We are recognizing every element. The ceremonial lodge is a temple, and like many of which we have heard during the years of these Eranos lectures, is an image of the universe in the form of a circle. "We have established here the center of the earth", the old Medicine Man explained, "and this center, which in reality is everywhere, is the dwelling place of Wakan Tanka[34]." Can this figure be a counterpart of the circle of Nicholas Cusanus ,whose circumference is nowhere and whose center is everywhere, the circle of the spirit? It is amazing to catch an echo of *this* thought from the lips of an old warrior of the Sioux.

Shall we then join our voice to those who write of a great Perennial Philosophy, which has been the one eternally true wisdom of the human

[33] Ibid., p. 5, note 4.
[34] Ibid., p. 108.

race, from time out of mind? Or shall we hold, rather, to the answer of the nineteenth-century anthropologists—Bastian, for example, Tylor and Frazer—who attributed such parallels to something rather psychological than metaphysically substantial: "the effect", as Frazer formulated the idea, "of similar causes acting alike on the similar constitution of the human mind in different countries and under different skies[35]"?

We note the formula four times seven, giving twenty-eight supports of the universe; the numbers four and seven being standard symbols of totality in the iconographies of both the Orient and the Occident: and this game of sacred numbers itself is a highly significant common trait. One of the twenty-eight is the pivot of the universe. The number surrounding it then is twenty-seven: three times nine: three times three times three. We think of Dr. Jung's numerous discussions of the symbolism of the four and three. We think of the nine choirs of angels, three times three, that surround and celebrate the central throne of the Trinity. The number four recurs in the clockwise circumambulation, now associated not only with the four directions but also with the life stages of the individual, so that the symbolism is being applied both to the macrocosm and to the microcosm: the two being tied by the number twenty-eight to the cycle of the moon, which dies and is resurrected and is therefore the cycle of renewal. Furthermore, the buffalo has twenty-eight ribs and is therefore himself a counterpart of the moon. Do not the buffaloes return every year, miraculously renewed, like the moon? We think of the Moon Bull of the archaic Near East, whose image appeared on the harps in the Royal Tombs of Ur: the animal symbol of the moon god, Sin, after whom Mount Sinai was named, so that it should represent the cosmic mountain at the center of the world. At the foot of that mountain—as we know—the High Priest, Aaron, conducted a festival of the golden calf, which Moses then committed to the fire, ground to bits, mixed with water, and caused the people to drink, in a kind of inverse communion meal[36]—reminding us of the killing, roasting, and eating of the young Marind-anim of which I spoke in the last hour.

[35] JAMES G. FRAZER, *The Golden Bough,* one-volume edition, New York 1922, p. 386.
[36] *Exodus* 32:1–20.

Only after this sacrifice did Moses receive, on the mountain top, where the heaven god meets the goddess Earth, the full assignment of the law and the promise of the Promised Land—not for himself (for he was now, himself, to be the sacrifice), but for the people. When he came down from the mountain the skin of his face shone like the moon, so that he had to wear a veil when he was before the people, like the archaic kings of the Moon Bull[37]. In the mythology of Christ, three days in the tomb, crucified and resurrected, there is implicit the same lunar symbolism. The Sacrificial Bull: the Sacrificial Lamb: the Cosmic Buffalo! Their symbology is perfectly interpreted by this old Medicine Man of the Sioux when he declares that the buffalo is symbolic of the universe in its temporal, lunar aspect, dying yet ever renewed, but also, in its twenty-eighth rib, of the Great Spirit, which is eternal.

Chief Standing Hollow Horn was seated at the west of the lodge, the place of honor, because there he faced the door, the east, from which comes the light, representing wisdom, and this illumination a leader must possess. The beautiful woman came before him and, lifting the bundle from her back, said to him: "Behold this bundle and always love it; for it is holy. No impure man should ever see it. Within there is a very holy pipe with which you are to send your voices to your Father and Grandfather."

She drew forth the pipe and with it a round stone, which she placed upon the ground. Lifting the pipe, with its stem to the sky, she said: "With this pipe you will walk upon the Earth; for the Earth is your Mother and Grandmother. Every step taken upon her should be a prayer. The bowl is of red pipestone: it is the Earth. Carved upon it is a buffalo calf, who represents all the quadrupeds living upon your Mother. The pipe stem is of wood, representing all that grows upon the Earth. And these twelve feathers, hanging here, where the stem enters the bowl, are feathers of the spotted eagle. They represent that eagle and all the winged things of the air.

"When you smoke this pipe all these things join you, everything in the

---

[37] Ibid., 34: 29–35.

universe, and they send their voices to your Father and Grandfather, the Great Spirit. When you pray with this pipe you pray for all things and all pray with you[38]."

The proper use of the pipe, as told by the old Medicine Man, Black Elk, requires that it should be identified with both the universe and oneself. A live coal is taken from the fire and the keeper of the pipe then places upon it a bit of sweet-grass that he has lifted four times to heaven with a prayer. "Within this grass", runs the prayer, "is the earth, this great island. Within it is my Grandmother, my Mother, and all creatures who walk in a holy manner. The fragrance of this grass will cover the universe. O Wakan Tanka, my Grandfather, be merciful to all."

The bowl of the pipe then is held over the burning grass in such a way that the smoke enters it, passing through the stem and coming out the end, which is directed toward heaven. "In this way", explained Black Elk, "Wakan Tanka is the first to smoke and by this act the pipe is purified[39]."

The pipe then is filled with tobacco that has been offered in the six directions: to the west, north, east, and south, then to heaven, then to earth. "In this manner", the old man said, "the whole universe is placed in the pipe[40]." Finally, the man who fills the pipe should identify it with himself. There is a prayer in which this identity is described:

> These people [says the prayer] had a pipe,
> Which they made to be their body.
>
> O my Friend, I have a pipe that I have made
>   to be my body;
> If you also make it to be your body,
> You shall have a body free from all causes of death.
>
> Behold the joint of the neck, they said,
> *That* I have made to be the joint of my own neck.
>
> Behold the mouth of the pipe,
> *That* I have made to be my mouth.
>
> Behold the right side of the pipe,
> *That* I have made to be the right side of my body.

---

[38] BROWN, op. cit., pp. 3–7.
[39] Ibid, p. 23.
[40] Ibid., p. 25.

Behold the spine of the pipe,
That I have made to be my own spine.

Behold the left side of the pipe,
That I have made to be the left side of my body.

Behold the hollow of the pipe,
That I have made to be the hollow of my body.

... use the pipe as an offering in your supplications,
And your prayers will be readily granted[41].

This holy game of purifying the pipe, expanding the pipe to include the universe, identifying oneself with the pipe, and then igniting it in symbolic sacrifice of the cosmos—macro- and microcosm—is a ritual act of the kind that we know from the Vedic Brahmanic rituals, where the altar and every implement of the sacrifice is allegorically associated both with the universe and with the individual. This ritual of the pipe is in precisely the same spirit.

Moreover, we now learn that the feathers on the pipe are of the spotted eagle, which is the highest flying bird in North America and therefore equivalent to the sun. Its feathers are the solar rays—and their number is twelve, which is the number, exactly, that we too associate with the cycle of the sun in our twelve months of the solar year and signs of the zodiac. There is a verse in one of the sacred songs of the Sioux, which says:

The Spotted Eagle is coming to carry me away.

Do we not think of the Greek myth of Ganymede carried away by Zeus, who came to him in the form of an eagle? "Birds", declares Dr. Jung in one of his dissertations on the process of individuation, "are thoughts and flights of the mind.... The eagle denotes the heights ... it is a well-known alchemistic symbol. Even the *lapis*, the *rebis* (made out of two parts, and thus often hermaphroditic, as a coalescence of Sol and Luna) is frequently represented with wings, in this way standing for premonition—intuition. All these symbols in the last analysis depict the

---

[41] FRANCIS LA FLESCHE, *War Ceremony and Peace Ceremony of the Osage Indians,* Bulletin No. 101, Bureau of American Ethnology, Washington, D.C., 1939, pp. 62–63; cited by BROWN, op. cit., p. 21.

state of affairs that we call the self, in its role of transcending consciousness[42]."

Such a reading certainly accords with the part played by our spotted eagle in the rites of the North American tribes. It explains, also, the wearing of eagle feathers. They are counterparts of the golden rays of a European crown. They are the rays of the spiritual sun, which the warrior, like the hunter, typifies in his life. Furthermore—as we have been told—their number in the war bonnet is twenty-eight, the number of the lunar cycle of temporal death and renewal, so that here Sol and Luna have been joined.

There can be no doubt whatsoever but this legend of the Sioux is fashioned of the same materials, precisely, as the great mythologies of the Old World—Europe, Africa and Asia. The parallels on every level, both in imagery and in sense, are far too numerous and too subtle to be the consequence of mere accident.—And we are not yet finished!

For when the holy woman before chief Standing Hollow Horn had told him how to use the pipe, she touched its bowl to the round stone that she had placed upon the ground. "You will be bound by this pipe", she said, "to your Father and Grandfather, your Mother and Grandmother."

The Great Spirit, the old Medicine Man explained, is our Father and Grandfather; the Earth our Mother and Grandmother. As Father and Mother they are the producers of all things, but as Grandfather and Grandmother they are beyond our understanding[43].

These are the two modes of considering God that Rudolf Otto has termed the "rational" and the "ineffable": the same that are called in India Saguṇa and Nirguṇa Brahman: the Absolute with qualities and without.

"This rock", the holy woman continued, "is of the same red stone as the bowl of the pipe: it is the Earth—your Mother and Grandmother. It is red: you, too, are red; and the Great Spirit has given you a red road."

---

[42] CARL G. JUNG, *The Integration of the Personality,* Farrar & Rinehart, Inc., New York and Toronto 1939, p. 189.

[43] BROWN, op. cit., pp. 5–6, notes 6 and 7.

The red road is the road of purity and life. The various Indian nations have many names for this road. The Navaho call it the "Pollen Path of Beauty". Its opposite, the black road, is followed by those "who are distracted, ruled by the senses, and live rather for themselves than for their people[44]." This was the road followed by the man at the opening of the story, who was consumed by snakes. And so we notice now that even the ethical polarity that we recognize between the bird and serpent as allegoric of the winged flight of the spirit and the earth-bound commitment of the passions, here too is suggested.

"These seven circles that you see upon the red stone", the woman said, "represent the seven rites in which the pipe will be used. Be good to this gift. With it, your people will increase and there will come to them all that is good." She described the rites and then turned to leave. "I am departing now, but I shall look back upon your people in every age; for, remember, in me there are four ages: and at the end I shall return."

Passing around the lodge in the sunwise direction, she left, but after walking a little distance, looked back and sat down. When she got up again, the people were amazed to see that she had turned into a young red and brown buffalo calf. The calf walked a little distance, lay down and rolled, looked back at the people, and when she got up was a white buffalo. This buffalo walked a little distance, rolled upon the ground, and when it rose was black. The black buffalo walked away, and when it was far from the people turned, bowed to each of the four directions, and disappeared over the hill[45].

The wonderful woman thus had been the feminine aspect of the cosmic buffalo itself: the earthly buffalo-calf represented on the red pipe bowl as well as its mother, the white buffalo, and its grandmother, the black. And she had gone to be resumed in her eternal portion, having rendered to man those sacred visible things and thoughts by which he was to be joined to his own eternity, which is here and now, within him and all things, in the living world. Let us try to follow her to her source.

[44] Ibid., p. 7, note 10.
[45] Ibid., pp. 7–9.

Let us follow, first, down the well of the past—the deep well of history and prehistory; for actually, a good deal is now known concerning the history of our North American tribes and their mythologies. We know, for example, that the Sioux were not always hunters of the buffalo, dwelling on the great plains. In the sixteenth century they lived among the lakes and marshes of the upper Mississippi, in the heavily wooded regions of Minnesota and Wisconsin, traveling mainly in bark canoes. They were a tribe of the forest, not of the plains, and knew practically nothing of the buffalo[46]. The White Buffalo woman cannot possibly have been a factor in their mythology at that time.

However, many of the other elements of this myth can have been known to them from of old: for example, the idea of the four ages and the lunar cycle, the ritual of the holy pipe and of the cosmic ceremonial lodge; that is to say, all of those elements that we have been equating with those known to our own tradition, and which belong rather to the world of the plant than to that of the hunt. In fact, to press the problem further, I should say that much of what we have heard in this myth suggests even the more complex, celestially oriented myths of the high civilizations, with their great play upon the numbers 3 and 4, 7, 12, and 28, their ethical themes and developed metaphysics.

We are not surprised, therefore, to learn that before the Sioux reached their northern forest station at the headwaters of the Mississippi, where they paddled their delicate bark canoes on the woodland lakes and rivers of the north, they had inhabited a more southerly sector of the long Mississippi valley[47], where the inhabitants were by no means merely hunters. For about two thousand years influences had been entering the Mississippi valley from Mexico[48], where a high civilization was flourishing, based on agriculture, governing its festival year by an astronomically correct calendar, and possessing cities that amazed the Spaniards

---

[46] GEORGE E. HYDE, *Red Cloud's Folk, A History of the Oglala Sioux,* University of Oklahoma Press, Norman, Oklahoma, 1936.

[47] Loc. cit.

[48] GORDON R. WILLEY and PHILIP PHILLIPS, *Method and Theory in American Archaeology,* University of Chicago Press, Chicago 1958, pp. 158–66.

when they arrived, comparable in size, grandeur, and sophistication, to the greatest in the Orient. The use of tobacco in the holy pipe—which is not a wild, but cultivated plant—should have let us know that the ritual could not have been originally of hunters. Furthermore, the Sioux themselves were not merely hunters. They planted maize, squash, and lima beans, and these, like tobacco, had come to the Mississippi valley from the south.

Let me name for you a few of the plants cultivated in South and Middle America before the coming of Columbus, so that you may judge of the force there of the agricultural principle and wonder, perhaps, what the Europeans can have been eating at that time besides bread, venison, and wine. For what would French cooking be without the *pomme de terre*? The potato was first developed in Chile, Bolivia, and Peru. What would Italian cooking be without tomato sauce? Tomatoes were developed in Mexico and Guatemala. Think of Spain without chili-peppers, Switzerland without chocolate, Western civilization without rubber, the modern world without tobacco! Tobacco was first brought to Europe in 1558 by Francisco Fernandes, who had been sent by Philip II of Spain to investigate the products of Mexico. The domesticated turkey also was brought to Europe at that time. In all, some fifty or sixty varieties of domesticated plants were first developed in pre-Columbian America, including maize, squash, the lima bean, pineapple, peanut and avocado, kidney bean, pumpkin, watermelon, papaya, and sweet potato[49].

More astonishing, however, is the fact that as early as 1000 B.C. an Asiatic cotton was being grown in Peru, together with a type of gourd—the bottle gourd—which had also been imported from Southeast Asia by way of a trans-Pacific voyage[50]. Furthermore, as Professor Jensen

---

[49] CARL O. SAUER, *Cultivated Plants of South and Central America,* in: "Handbook of South American Indians" (ed. JULIAN H. STEWARD), Bulletin 143, Bureau of American Ethnology, Washington, D.C., Vol. VI, 1950, pp. 487–543.

[50] Cf. GEORGE F. CARTER, *Plants across the Pacific,* "American Antiquity", Vol. XVIII, No. 3, Part 2, January, 1953, pp. 62–63 and 71, and FREDERICK JOHNSON, *Radiocarbon Dating,* "Memoirs of the American Society for American Archaeology", No. 8, Salt Lake City 1951, p. 10, Sample No. 321; also, SAUER, op. cit., pp. 506 and 537–38.

pointed out in his Eranos lecture of ten years ago, to which I have already alluded, even on the primitive mesolithic level there is abundant evidence of an equatorial cultural continuum, extending all the way from West Africa eastward, through India and Southeast Asia, across the Pacific to America; and I can assure you that from year to year evidence accumulates re-enforcing this hypothesis—which is now practically a proven fact. And one of the characteristic elements of this *Kulturkreis* is precisely the myth of the killed and buried plant divinity.

In other words, the basic myth of the planting mythology that we considered in the last hour has been identified in a continuous series of transformations running from the African Ivory Coast to the Amazon. And in each region it has been adjusted to the local vegetation. In primitive Indonesia it is referred to the banana, coconut, and yam; in Mexico to maize; in Brazil to .manioc; in ancient Ur it was applied to wheat; in Japan to rice.

Can the legends of the Sioux, then, have been touched by this tradition?

It would be amazing had they not. For at the time of their residence in the central Mississippi valley there was an intensive concentration here of agricultural villages with immense, rectangular temple mounds arranged around central plazas, towns of several hundred souls, crops of maize, squash, and beans, spiritual as well as secular governors, and recondite religious iconographies. This so-called Middle Mississippi Culture had struck its roots, apparently, as early as the fifth century B.C. and culminated in the fifteenth A.D., with extensions eastward to the Atlantic, westward into Arkansas, and north through Illinois[51]. The culture level was about equivalent to that of France at the time of Vercingetorix, the period of Caesar's Gallic Wars. Furthermore, the temple mounds let us know that the influence of Mexico was direct and of considerable force.

But we have evidence today of a direct impact on the nuclear centers of Peru and Middle America from China and Southeast Asia, commenc-

---

[51] WILLEY and PHILLIPS, op. cit., pp. 163–70.

ing at least as early as the eighth century B.C., when China was already
halfway through its great period of the Chou dynasty, and continuing
perhaps to the twelfth century A.D., when the fabulous—but ephemeral
—Khmer civilization of Ankor can be shown to have directly influenced
the Mayan architecture of Chiapas, Tobasco, Campeche, Piedras Negras,
and the Toltec city of the fabled King Quetzalcoatl[52].

It is entirely possible, therefore, that every one of those elements that
have impressed us in the mythology of the Sioux are actually consti-
tuents of that same great mythological complex of the agriculturally
based high civilizations from which our own mythology is derived and
that, consequently, they do not illustrate any generally valid archetypology of the psyche but an archetypology only of the high civilizations—which, as we know from the archaeology of the past few decades,
derive, one and all, from the Mesopotamian mother of civilizations, into
whose secrets we have glanced in the Royal Tombs of Ur.

On the other hand, the enveloping atmosphere of the legend is very
different from that of the myths, either of the primitive planters, or of
the higher agricultural civilizations. Compared with the Blackfoot origin
legend of the buffalo dance and All Comrades society, it immediately
reveals itself to be of the same order. These two tribes, the Blackfeet and
the Sioux, were enemies and of very different racial stock—the Blackfeet
were Algonquins, the Sioux, Siouan. Yet their legends of the origin of
their buffalo rites contain the same motifs. In both cases, the rites are
described as having been brought to the tribe from the animals themselves, by the buffalo maid or buffalo wife. In the Blackfoot variant she
was a woman of the tribe, in that of the Sioux, the female aspect of the
cosmic buffalo itself. Many more variants of this theme have been col-
lected from the tribes of the great plains: and although all of them reveal
a strong infusion of planting motifs, the basic stance remains shaman-

---

[52] GORDON F. ECKHOLM, *A Possible Focus of Asiatic Influence in the Late Classic
Cultures of Mesoamerica*, "Memoirs of the Society of American Archaeology", Vol.
XVIII, No. 3, Part 2, January, 1953, pp. 72–89; also, ibid., *The New Orientation
toward Problems of Asiatic-American Relationships*, in: *New Interpretations of
Aboriginal American Culture History*, "75th Anniversary Volume of the Anthro-
pological Society of Washington", Washington, D.C., 1955, pp. 95–109.

istic. The rites are not, for the most part, referred to a mythological age of mythological ancestors, but were derived from visionary encounters with the Animal Masters or Master Animals.

There is now plenty of evidence to show that on the buffalo plains of North America there survived to the end of the nineteenth century, and even somewhat into the twentieth, a powerful late formation of truly paleolithic culture forms. There is a variety of North American stone spear point, called the Clovis Point, for which a radiocarbon date of 35,000 B.C. plus has been established, and which is consistently associated with remains of the mammoth. Another, the Folsom Point, belongs to about 8,000 B.C. and is found with the remains of an extinct bison. The paleolithic grottoes of southern France and northern Spain, you will recall, are dated from *c.* 35,000 to 10,000 B.C. But points of these kinds continued to be fashioned on the plains of North America well into the first millennium A.D.

It is really an amazing, thrilling experience for anyone acquainted with the customs of the North American tribes to enter one of those French or Spanish grottoes. The caves were not domestic sites, but sanctuaries of the men's rites: rituals of the hunt and of initiation. They are dangerous and absolutely dark. And the pictures on the rocky walls are never near the entrances but always deep within—placed frequently with an amazing sense for dramatic impact. The painted animals, living forever in eternal darkness, beyond the tick of time, are the germinal, deathless herds of the cosmic night, from which those on earth—which appear and disappear in continuous renewal—proceed, and back to which they return. And whenever human forms appear among them, they are shamans, wearing the costumes that Indian shamans wear to this day.

One sees, also, many silhouetted handprints—the hands of the hunters of those times; and from a number of them certain finger joints are missing. Our Indians, too, chopped off their finger joints as offerings to the sun, or to Wakan Tanka—with prayers for power and success.

In a few of the caves, deep and special chambers have been found, where rites of exceptional power must have been celebrated. In the grotto of Trois-Frères, for example, there is a long, very narrow, tubelike passage—a long flume hardly two feet high—through which you have to crawl and wriggle on your belly for about fifty yards, until, at last, you come to a large chamber with animal forms engraved everywhere on the walls, and among them, directly opposite and facing the very difficult passage through which you have painfully arrived, is the celebrated Sorcerer of Trois-Frères: a dancing shaman, with the antlers of a deer, a beard flowing to his chest, two big, round eyes staring at you, the body and front paws of a lion, tail of a wolf, and legs of a man.

At Lascaux, in a kind of crypt or lower chamber, there is the picture of a shaman lying on the ground in a shamanistic trance, wearing the mask and costume of a bird. His shaman staff is beside him, bearing on its top the figure of a bird. And, standing before him, is a great bison bull, struck from behind, mortally, by a lance.

And in the cave Tuc d'Audoubert there is a little chamber entered only by a very small hole, through which a man can scarcely squeeze. Within are two clay statuettes in high relief—unique in paleolithic art— representing a bison bull and cow, the bull mounting the cow, while on the ground are the footprints of a dancer, who had been dancing on his heels, in imitation of the hoofs of the buffalo, whose song, as we have heard, is slow and solemn, and whose dance step is ponderous and deliberate. And there were also in this chamber a number of phallic forms, roughly modeled in clay.

Ladies and Gentlemen: I think that we can now presume to say that we have beheld our goddess Buffalo in divine connubium, and know from what far land and time, beyond their ken, the very beautiful woman came whom the two Sioux Indians saw on the North American plain. For there can be no question concerning the land of origin of the hunting tribes of North America. The vast area of the paleolithic Great Hunt, which stretched in a single sweep from the Pyrenees to Lake Baikal, in Siberia, actually went on to the Mississippi. And the Indians, who came from northern Asia in many waves, brought with them the rites and hunting methods of that world.

These rites and methods, that is to say, were not separately invented in Europe, Asia, and America, but carried from one area to the other. And the *mythogenetic zone,* the primary area of origin of the myths, was certainly the Old World, not the New. North America was, therefore, not a primary zone, but a *zone of diffusion,* an area to which the myths and rites were transferred.

However, a transfer of this kind is never inert. There are two processes of secondary creativity that come into play when mythologies are transferred, and I should like to speak of them briefly, for just a moment.

The first we may term *land-taking.* In the case, for example, of the primitive planting myth that we discussed in the last hour, the mythological being who was sacrificed and now lives again in the food plants is associated in Brazil with manioc, in Japan with rice, and in Mexico with maize. It is everywhere the same myth, the same mystery play, but in each province the local landscape is its theater and the local animals and plants become its actors. Land-taking, then, is the act of taking spiritual possession of a newly entered land with all its elements, by assimilation to a myth already carried in one's heart in the way of a continuing culture. We are not to suppose that in every province of the tropical continuum the one same myth was separately developed.

The second process that I would like to mention is the one that Professor Eliade illustrated in his lecture on the Cargo Cults of Melanesia; namely, *acculturation.* Here, motifs from an alien culture complex are received into a native tradition by a process of syncretistic assimilation. And the rapidity with which such a process can take effect—as we have seen—is amazing. In the Cargo Cults, like a flash fire, the new inspiration reached far beyond the colonial culture zone, far into the bush, into the wild country of men who had never seen a white man.

And so it was of old, also, in America, when the mythologies of Mexico penetrated the Mississippi: the motifs of the higher mythology were syncretistically assimilated by the northern hunters and applied to their own fields of myth and rite. The Sioux and Pawnee, for example, assimilated to their image of the Master Buffalo the Mexican astronomical myth of the Four Ages—the same four cosmic ages that were known to Hesiod as the ages of Gold, Silver, Bronze, and Iron, and to India as the cycle of four *yugas,* during the course of which (it is declared) the cow of virtue lost with each *yuga* one leg—standing first on four legs, then on three legs, then on two, and now, in our own miserable age, on one.

The Pawnee and the Sioux declare that their Cosmic Buffalo, the father and grandfather of the universe, stands at the cosmic gate through which the game animals pour into the world and back through which they go when they are slain, to be reborn. And in the course of the cycle of the four world ages, with the passage of each year, that buffalo sheds one hair, and with the passage of each age, one leg[53].

The resemblance of this image to that of India is amazing; and the more so when compared with a tale from the *Brahmavaivarta Purāṇa* which Heinrich Zimmer recounts at the opening of his volume on *Myths and Symbols in Indian Art and Civilization*. There, the Lord of the Universe, the god Shiva, whose animal is the white bull Nandi, appears in the form of an old yogi named Hairy, who has on his chest a circular patch of hair from which one hair falls at the end of each cosmic cycle. At the end of a Brahma year of such cosmic cycles all the hairs are gone and the whole universe dissolves into the night sea, the Ocean of Milk, to be renewed.

Who will say by what miracle—whether of history or of psychology— these two homologous images came into being, the one in India and the other in North America? It is possible that one of the paths of diffusion just described may have been followed. However, it is also possible that the two images were developed independently by some process of *convergence*, as an "effect", to use Frazer's words, "of similar causes acting alike on the similar constitution of the human mind in different countries and under different skies"; for in India, too, there was a meeting of animal and plant cultures when the Aryans arrived with their flocks in the Dravidian agricultural zone. Analogous processes may have been set in play—as in two separate alchemical retorts.

So that we must now confess that our tracking down of the goddess Buffalo may have brought us face to face with a problem not of history

[53] BROWN, op. cit., p. 6, note 8, and p. 9, note 15; also, GEORGE A. DORSEY, *The Pawnee: Mythology* (Part I), The Carnegie Institute of Washington, Washington, D.C., 1906, p. 134.

only, but of psychology as well. We have perhaps broken beyond the walls of time and space, and should ask by what psychological as well as historical laws these primitive myths and their counterparts in the higher cultures might have been formed.

There is, however, no such thing as an uncommitted psychology of man *qua* "Man", abstracted from a specific historical field. For, as Dr. Portmann has pointed out to us in his lectures in this hall, the human infant is born (biologically speaking) a year too soon, completing in the social sphere a development that other species accomplish within the womb; in fact, developing in the social sphere precisely those powers most typically human: upright posture, rational thought, and speech. Man—as "Man"—develops in a manner that is simultaneously biological and social, and this development continues through adolescence— in fact, through life.

Moreover, whereas the instinct system of the animal is relatively inflexible, fixed, stereotyped, according to species, that of man is not so, but open to imprint *(Prägung)* and impression. The Innate Releasing Mechanisms of the human central nervous system, through which man's instincts are triggered to action, respond to Sign Stimuli that are not fixed for all time and general to the species, but vary from culture to culture, century to century, individual to individual, according to imprints indelibly registered during the long course of a sociologically conditioned childhood. And if I have read aright the works of Dr. Portmann and his colleagues: there has not yet been identified a single triggering image, a single Sign Stimulus, that can be firmly verified as innate to the human psyche.

How, then, shall we rest secure in any theory of psychological archetypes based upon our own culturally conditioned mode of responses, or upon a study of the myths and symbols of our own tradition, or even a comparative study of that large complex of primitive planting and higher agricultural traditions, which, as I have just indicated, are both historically and prehistorically related to our own?

We have to realize that the walls have lately been knocked from around all mythologies—every single one of them—by the findings and works of modern scientific discovery. The four ages, the four points of the compass, the four elements! What can those mean to man today, in the light of what we are learning? Today we have ninety-six elements, and the number is still growing. The old soul and the new universe—the old microcosm and the new macrocosm—do not match; and the disproportion is about equivalent to that of 4 to 96. No wonder if a lot of us are nervous! The little tower of Babel, which to some in its day seemed to be threatening God in his heaven, we see now surpassed many times in every major city of the world, and rockets fly where once the angels sang. One cannot *tutoyer* God any more: the mystery is infinite, both without and within. That is the *tremendum* that our modern mind—this flower of creation—has revealed for us to absorb, and it cannot be willed or walled away by any system of archaic feeling. It will not be screened from us, nor we protected, by any organization of archaic images. There has not yet been identified a single image that can be definitely guaranteed as innate to man.

And so, we are compelled to face our problem of the imagery of myth largely from a historical point of view, after all. That wonderful sentence of Charles Darwin's that Dr. Benz quoted the other day, and which apparently shocked Darwin himself, where it was suggested that the image of God might be only an imprint impressed upon the mind of man through centuries of teaching, fits the case precisely—at least as far as anything but faith can tell us. But faith itself would then be only a reflex of the imprint.

So let us briefly review, in these closing minutes of the hour, a few of those inevitable imprints to which the human individual, no matter where he may have developed, must always have been subject. These we may number, I believe, among the sources of those archetypal images that are found in all mythologies, variously arranged. They supply at least one series of those Sign Stimuli by which our human energies are triggered to action and organized for life as the instincts of the beasts by the Sign Stimuli of their species: those energy releasing signs by which man is struck and moved, as it were, from within.

The first of such imprintings are, of course, those to which the infant is subjected in its earliest years. These have been extensively discussed in the literature of psychoanalysis, and may be sketchily summarized about as follows: (1) those of the birth trauma and its emotional effects; (2) those of the mother and father images in their benevolent and malevolent transformations; (3) those associated with the infant's interest in its own excrement and the measures of discipline imposed upon it in relation to this context; (4) those of the child's sexual researches and acquisition of a castration complex (whether in the male or in the female mode); and then, (5) the constellation of these imprints now generally known by the name of Oedipus. There can be little doubt that no matter where in the world an infant may ever have been born, as long as the nuclear unit of human life has been a father, mother, and child, the maturing consciousness has had to come to a knowledge of its world through the medium of this heavily loaded, biologically based triangle of love and aggression, desire and fear, dependency, command, and urge for release.

But now, in every primitive society on earth—whether of the hunting or of the planting order—these inevitable imprints and conceptions of infancy are filled with new associations, rearranged and powerfully re-imprinted, under the most highly emotional circumstances, in the puberty rites, the rites of initiation, to which every young male (and often every female too) is subjected. That long flume in the paleolithic grotto of Trois-Frères, with the vivid image of the dancing, staring sorcerer in the chamber to which it led, must have been employed in such a rite. A fundamental motif in the puberty rites of many lands is that of death to infancy and rebirth to manhood, and this grotto shows every sign of having been used for just such an effect. Moreover, in these rites, the child's body is painfully altered—through circumcision, subincision, ritual defloration, clitoridectomy, tattooing, scarification, or what not; so that there is no childhood to which the child can now return. And through these forceful rearrangements of the references of the father image, mother image, birth idea, etc., the reflex system of the whole psyche is transformed. The infantile system of responses is erased and the energies carried forward, away from childhood, away from the attitude of dependency that is a function of the long infancy characteristic of our species—on to adulthood, engagement in the local tasks of man- and womanhood, to an attitude of adult responsibility and a sense of integration with the local group.

A neurotic, then, can be defined as one in whom this initiation has failed of its effect, so that in him those socially organized Sign Stimuli that carry others on to their adult tasks continue to refer only back- ward—to the imprint system of the infant. The mother image then is experienced only as a reference to the human mother of one's child- hood, not to the life-producing, disciplining, and supporting aspect of the world (which is our Mother and Grandmother), and the father is not Wakan Tanka, but that "undemonstrative relative", as James Joyce terms him, "who settles our hash bill for us". All attempts, therefore, to interpret myths through a study of the imagery of neurotics neces- sarily run the risk of failing to consider precisely that aspect of mythol- ogy which is distinctive, namely, its power to carry people *away* from childhood—from dependency—on to responsibility.

Furthermore, the peculiar interests of adulthood differ radically from one society to another, and since it is a primary function of myth and ritual in traditional societies to shape youngsters into adults and then to hold the adults to their given roles, mythology and ritual, in as far as they serve this local, moral, ethical aim, cannot be called functions of any generally valid human psychology, but only of local history and sociology.

Professor A. R. Radcliffe-Brown of Cambridge University has well discussed this aspect of our subject in his work on the pigmies of the Andaman Islands, where he writes as follows:

"(1) A society depends for its existence on the presence in the minds of its members of a certain system of sentiments by which the conduct of the individual is regulated in conformity with the needs of the society. (2) Every feature of the social system itself and every event or object that in any way affects the well-being or the cohesion of the society becomes an object of this system of sentiments. (3) In human society the sentiments in question are not innate but are developed in the individual by the action of the society upon him. (4) The ceremonial customs of a society are a means by which the sentiments in question are given collective expression on appropriate occasions. (5) The ceremonial (i.e. collective) expression of any sentiment serves both to maintain it at the requisite degree of intensity in the mind of the individual and to transmit it from one generation to another. Without such expression the sentiments involved could not exist[54]."

Mythology, in short, is not a natural, spontaneous production of the individual psyche, but a socially controlled reorganization of the imprints of childhood, so contrived that the Sign Stimuli moving the individual will conduce to the well-being of the local culture, and that local culture alone. What is effective, as well as distinctive, in every mythology, therefore, is its locally ordered architecture, not the bricks (the infantile imprints and their affects) of which this structure is composed: and this architecture, this organization, differs significantly, according to place, time, and culture stage.

However, there is one more aspect and great function of mythology to be noted—and here we find ourselves moving away from the local back to general human terms; for man has not only to be led by myth from the infantile attitude of dependency to the system of sentiments of the local group, but also, in adulthood, to be prepared to face the mystery of death: to absorb the *mysterium tremendum;* since man, like no other animal, not only knows that he is killing when he kills, but also knows that he too will die; and his old age, furthermore, like his infancy, is a lifetime in itself, as long as the whole life span of many a beast.

But this role and function of myth was already treated in the first hour, and so, I shall now add only one remark. I shall observe only that even if the view of the Freudian school is correct and the experience of dread before this *tremendum* is finally but a reflex of the child's Oedipal dread of the father and thus an imprint not of later but of earlier life, nevertheless, it is an imprint of peculiar metaphysical moment. For the susceptibility of the human mind to this experience is what has

---

[54] A. R. RADCLIFFE-BROWN, *The Andaman Islanders,* Cambridge University Press, 1933, pp. 233–34.

alienated man from nature and made it necessary for all mythologies to serve the one paramount task, throughout the world, of wooing *das kranke Tier* (to quote Nietzsche) back to life.

It lay beyond the program of the present paper to review in the higher mythologies the interplay of the two primitive stances to this dread that were discussed in the first hour: that of the hunt (negative toward death and positive toward ego) and that of the tropical planters (negative toward ego and positive toward death). Yet, surely, it is apparent, even on first glance, that in the Western, Judeo-Christian phases of the post-neolithic development of civilization a masculine resistance to the mystery of death and generation has come forcefully into play. For the Messianic idea, which plays such a role here, is nothing if not a refutation of the world as it now stands and a prayer for something better in a timeless time to come, whereas, in the primary primitive planting mythology, the day of the Messiah is now: here and now. The godhead, or godly power, lives already in all things, because dead to itself. It is in us. And we are *It* in as far as we, too, are dead to ego. There is nothing to come. There is nothing to change. This—right here and now—is It.

And throughout the world, wherever the feminine, submissive and mystical, in contrast to the masculine, ego-protective, magical system with its rites of conjuring has prevailed, we find in the myths no comprehension whatsoever of these patriarchal dreams of a happy day some time to come—but rather, a fierce, Dionysian rapture (which to the other side seems no less monstrous than life itself) wherein the cannibal feast of the life that lives on life and is ever-renewed, mightily—utterly careless of the individual: utterly careless of all rules of order—is celebrated with a shout and a howl. The primitive planting myth of life *in* death is subtly transformed, in the late, historical cultures, into one of life *as* death: and again that sense of alienation is returned to us, on the screen of a promise for the future. The primitive renewal, in contrast—whether of the hunters or of the planters—is ever present.

Hence, it is not surprising that in the present historical epoch of cultural death and renewal, nihilism and released spontaneity, when we are all again, like primitive man, feeling our way into a new world, a world as yet unknown (which, however, has come pouring out of our own arts and sciences), there is an appeal that has been felt by many of our creative minds in these primitive myths of a continuing creation, uncircumscribed, as yet, by any zodiac or an Alpha and Omega.

And so one more idea, now, in conclusion:

Some years ago Professor Portmann told us of a certain species of butterfly, the grayling *(Eumenis semele)*, the males of which assume the initiative in mating by pursuing a passing female in flight. And those little males generally prefer females of darker hue to lighter—to such a degree that if an artificial model of darker hue is presented than anything known to nature, the sexually motivated grayling male will pursue the work of art in preference to the darkest female of the living species. "Here we find", comments Dr. Portmann, "an 'inclination' that is not satisfied in nature, but which perhaps, one day, if inheritable darker mutations should appear, would play a role in the selection of mating partners. Who knows", he then asks, "whether such anticipations of particular Sign Stimuli ... may not represent one of the factors in the process of selection that determines the direction of evolution?[55]"

Stimuli of this kind, going beyond the offerings of nature yet triggering innate releasing mechanisms, are known as "supernormal sign stimuli", and, as this amusing little deception of the grayling shows, though nature responds to them, they are produced by art.

I am now suggesting that a mythology is a context of supernormal sign stimuli, produced by art for the government of nature. And these signs, through the ages, have been releasing, progressively—though frequently to our shock—the energies of the deepest secret of our being, which is, of course, the *mysterium tremendum.*

"There is a power called Sila", said an old Eskimo shaman from the remote rim of northernmost Alaska, "but Sila cannot be explained in so many words. It is a strong spirit, the upholder of the universe, of the weather, in fact all life on earth—so mighty that his speech to man comes not through ordinary words, but through storms, snowfall, rain

---

[55] ADOLF PORTMANN, *Die Bedeutung der Bilder in der lebendigen Energiewandlung,* "Eranos-Jahrbuch" XXI/1952, Rhein-Verlag, Zürich 1953, pp. 333–34.

showers, the tempests of the sea, through all the forces that man fears; or through sunshine, calm seas, or small, innocent playing children who understand nothing. When times are good, Sila has nothing to say to mankind. He has disappeared into his infinite nothingness and remains away as long as people do not abuse life but have respect for their daily food. No one has ever seen Sila. His place of sojourn is so mysterious that he is with us and infinitely far away at the same time[56]."

These words from the lips of an old fighter and man killer—who was no saint, let me assure you—I am citing as an envoi, to balance the historical stress of the body of my lecture. For in every time, in every culture, men have been born whose minds have broken past their culture horizon. Among the hunters, these have been the shamans, and their wisdom may, after all, be that of man *qua* Man.

"The only true wisdom", said the shaman Igjugarjuk, of whom I spoke to you in the last hour, "the only true wisdom lives far from mankind, out in the great loneliness, and it can be reached only through suffering. Privation and suffering alone can open the mind of a man to all that is hidden to others[57]."

And what, then, is the wisdom that is learned by the one who shatters within himself the fears that bind the others of his tribe to their little rites? What is the wisdom learned from Sila's voice?

"All that we know", said Najagneq, the shaman from the northern rim of the arctic, "is that the voice is gentle, like a woman's: a voice so fine and gentle that even children cannot become afraid. And what it says is: 'Be not afraid of the universe!'[58]"

How early in the history of mankind revelations of this order were received and recognized, we shall never know.

---

[56] H. OSTERMANN, *The Alaskan Eskimos, as Described in the Posthumous Notes of Dr. Knud Rasmussen,* "Report of the Fifth Thule Expedition 1921–24", Vol. X, No. 3, Nordisk Forlag, Copenhagen 1952, pp. 97–99.

[57] Ibid., p. 99.

[58] Ibid., p. 128.

MYTHS, DREAMS, RELIGION, PSYCHE . . .

Myths, Dreams, and Religion   JOSEPH CAMPBELL, ed.

Campbell compares the functions of mythology and art in "experiencing the mystery dimension of man's being"; Alan Watts lays out our primary Western myths, goading us toward their transformations; Norman O. Brown aphoristically catches Daphne in flight. Essays by David Miller, Ira Progoff, Owen Barfield, Stanley Hopper, Rollo May, Richard Underwood, and others further interlace myth, dream, poetry, philosophy and psychoanalysis, going to the roots of religious feeling in the soul of modern thought. (255 pp.)

The Self in Psychotic Process   JOHN WEIR PERRY

The author's therapy in the California Bay Area with acute episodes in young psychotic patients brought him national and international renown. The case of the young housewife diagnosed catatonic schizophrenic demonstrates the interpenetration of collective symbols and individual processes as they come to light in "breakdown" (Part One), and extends knowledge of the psyche by elucidating symbols of the Self (Part Two). This second edition includes a new preface by Dr. Perry, together with the original Foreword by C. G. Jung, scholarly apparatus, illustrations, and index. (xv, 184 pp.)

Waking Dreams   MARY WATKINS

Recovers the immeasurable riches of daydreams, active imagination, and imaginal others, showing the relevance of fantasy to the practice of psychotherapy, education, and the drama of individual lives. At once historical, critical, and clinical, this book takes one through both European and American approaches to the image, finally delivering the reader to a close look at his/her own relation to the imaginal world. (viii, 174 pp.)

Words as Eggs: Psyche in Language and Clinic   RUSSELL LOCKHART

Lockhart, a practicing Jungian analyst, examines a wide range of phenomena, including behavioral therapy, the psychology of cancer, the psyche of money and of words, Greek myth, alchemy, the unconscious and dreams, eros in relationships, film: *Deliverance*, and books: *Illness as Metaphor* and *Moby Dick*. Quietly passionate and urgently intent, this book belongs to the best tradition of depth psychology. (233 pp.)

Psyche and Death: Death-Demons in Folklore, Myths and Modern Dreams

                                                                  EDGAR HERZOG

Exhumes from fairytale and folklore the macabre variations of the archaic Death Image. In Part I, the author demonstrates that Death originally revealed itself in the guise of an animal—Wolf, Horse, Dog, Snake, and Bird. Today Death takes similar forms, appearing to human consciousness mainly through dreams. Part II, focusing on the dreams of patients undergoing analysis, links persons, scenes, and drama to the symbolic images and rites of the ancient past. Bibliography, indexes. (224 pp.)

Facing Apocalypse   N. O. BROWN, R. J. LIFTON et al.

Proceedings of a conference which met to give contour and features to "the end." Each approach—whether the peace activism of the poet Denise Levertov or the radical reflections on Islam by Norman O. Brown—*imagines* the nuclear devastation menacing the horizon so that it can reveal its meanings, thereby defusing its literal urgency. James Hillman invokes the God Mars to wake us up, while David Miller and Wolfgang Giegerich unveil the theological fantasies hidden in the "end of the world." (195 pp.)

Spring Publications • *P.O. Box 222069* • *Dallas, Texas 75222*